Original title:
Laughing Logs

Copyright © 2025 Creative Arts Management OÜ
All rights reserved.

Author: Jaxon Kingsley
ISBN HARDBACK: 978-1-80567-400-9
ISBN PAPERBACK: 978-1-80567-699-7

The Joy of Weathered Wood

In a forest where the trees play,
Old stumps giggle in a merry way.
Knots and grooves tell tales of cheer,
Whispering secrets for all to hear.

The branches sway with a playful tease,
While squirrels dance like they're on the breeze.
The bark wears a grin, full of delight,
As shadows cavort in the soft moonlight.

Woodland Whimsy Unleashed

Mighty oaks with their funny frown,
Wobble in tune, never wear a crown.
Acorns tumble with a pansy flair,
Each one's a jester, beyond compare.

Pinecones chatter, a nature's jest,
Under the sun, they wiggle the best.
Mossy patches hold laughter in store,
Where critters gather and stories pour.

The Cheerful Chorus of Cedars

Cedars sing with a rustling laugh,
As branches wave like a dancing staff.
Their needles shimmer, a bright parade,
In the soft sunlight, joyfully displayed.

The breeze carries giggles through the woods,
Tickling leaves in their leafy hoods.
Beneath their shade, mischief resides,
Where the woodland's jesters all coincide.

Treetop Tickles

Up high where the sky meets the green,
The canopies chuckle, a sight unseen.
Leaves quiver with glee, a joyous dance,
Inviting all creatures to join in the chance.

Branches play hopscotch with clouds above,
As sunlight drizzles like a warm hug.
Nature's laughter echoes down low,
In a woodland world where giggles flow.

The Lark in the Log

A lark perched high, with a wink and a grin,
Sings of a bark where the giggles begin.
Branches sway gently, dance with the breeze,
Tickling the leaves, as they play with ease.

Under the shade, a squirrel scrambles by,
With acorn hats and a glance to the sky.
Amidst ancient woods, tales of joy unfold,
In whispers of nature, a treasure of gold.

Merrily Meandering Paths

Around every twist, where the wildflowers bloom,
Footsteps go skipping, filled with perfume.
A stumble on roots leads to chuckles and cheer,
As mushrooms tease toes, 'Come dance over here!'

In playful disguise, a fox dips and dives,
Chasing the shadows where laughter thrives.
Paths twist and twirl with a wink and a nod,
Echoes of joy, where the weird and the odd.

The Whims of Nature's Giants

Tall trees with faces, they grin as they sway,
Whispering secrets in a whimsical way.
The smallest of critters, they join in the fun,
In this grand theater, all fuse into one.

Breezes carry chuckles, as they weave through the pines,
Caterpillars cartwheel on sun-dappled lines.
In a jolly parade, the forest confides,
Nature's great jesters, in laughter, they glide.

Echoes of Enchanted Timber

Beneath boughs that giggle, a doorway appears,
To realms where the bursts of bright laughter nears.
The logs whisper warmly, with stories to share,
Of revels and rambles that dance in the air.

Under the canopy, dreams twirl in delight,
The chorus of critters ignites the night bright.
With echoes of mirth making shadows that prance,
In the heart of the woods, we all take a chance.

Smiles and Sap

In the forest where the sunlight plays,
Trees whisper jokes in funny ways.
Barks do chuckle, leaves do grin,
They share the joy from deep within.

Roots wiggle like they know a tale,
Branches dance with a breezy gale.
Sap drips down with a giggly tune,
Nature's laughter under the moon.

The Hilarious Tangents of Twigs

Twigs twist and turn in wild spirals,
Each bend a quip, their humor viral.
They poke fun at the passing breeze,
While critters join in, as they please.

A squirrel stops by and cracks a grin,
As twigs tell tales where smiles begin.
Every snap brings a gasp and sigh,
In this wood, joy flutters high.

The Giggle of Gnarled Branches

Gnarled branches, a twisted crew,
Share secrets known to but a few.
Each creak and groan a playful jest,
In this hearty wood, they're all blessed.

The shadows dance on the forest floor,
While branches chuckle and want more.
Their laughter rings through the leafy maze,
Creating smiles in sunny rays.

Radiance in Reflection

Amidst the woods where the laughter flows,
Light reflects off the trees' fine prose.
A mirror of joy among the leaves,
Where every whisper a laugh receives.

Sunbeams tickle the trunks so stout,
While nature hums with a playful shout.
Smiles abound beneath the shade,
In this wood, happiness is made.

Merry Spirits in the Timber

In the woods where giggles play,
The branches dance, come what may.
Squirrels toss acorns with glee,
As whispers swirl through each tree.

A rustle here, a chuckle there,
The trunks wear smiles, a light affair.
Bunnies hop with jolly face,
In this merry, wooded place.

Nature's Silly Serenade

Breezes blow with cheeky flair,
Flowers chuckle, scents to share.
Birds exchange their comical calls,
As sunlight dances, laughter sprawls.

The leaves join in, a rustling cheer,
Nature's jesters, bright and clear.
A parade of whimsy, wild and free,
Singing joy from tree to tree.

Humorous Hues in the Heartwood

In layers deep, the colors grin,
Wooden hearts are light within.
Bark has stories, old and bold,
Ancient laughter to behold.

Winks of yellow, blushes bright,
Painting shadows in delight.
With every ring, a tale unfolds,
Of prancing spirits, young and old.

Frolicsome Knots and Twists

In every twist, a giggle hides,
The gnarled wood where fun abides.
Nature's tricks with every knot,
Bring forth laughter, joyful thought.

Branches bend in playful sway,
As critters dance and prance away.
Each creak and crack, a melody,
In this frolicsome symphony.

The Woodland's Whimsical Whispers

In the forest where giggles bloom,
Trees wear hats, dispelling gloom.
Squirrels dance, a cheeky spree,
Tickling winds, wild and free.

Frogs croak jokes on lily pads,
Rabbits grinning, oh so glad.
Mice play tricks in leafy shade,
Underneath the sun's cascade.

Branches sway with playful grace,
Nature's laughter in this place.
A deer winks, a sly delight,
As fireflies spark in the night.

With every rustle, joy's unveiled,
Whispers weaving, never pale.
In this realm of silly sights,
Wonders dance in dappled lights.

Jolly Jests in the Underbrush

Amidst the ferns, a chuckle stirs,
Chirping birds in feathery blurs.
Hedgehogs giggle, rolling 'round,
With acorns bouncing off the ground.

Bunnies hop in a measuring race,
Tails bobbing in a comical chase.
Bees buzz tales of sweet delight,
Joining in the fun in flight.

Mushrooms wear a cap so tall,
Pillowed sprouts, they catch the fall.
Insects tap their tiny shoes,
Creating rhythms in vibrant hues.

Whiskers twitch with every jest,
Nature's humor manifests.
In the underbrush, joy prevails,
Tales of laughter fill the trails.

Mirth Among the Moss

Softly nestled, greens collide,
Where chuckles live and secrets hide.
Tiny critters spark a cheer,
Mossy cushions cradle here.

Giggling streams with tippy toes,
Water sprites in gleeful flows.
A toad sings ballads, rich and grand,
While sunbeams twirl, hand in hand.

Rusty old logs share a grin,
As mushrooms sprout, thick and thin.
Branches twist in joyous play,
Nature's jesters, day by day.

In this thicket, laughter roams,
Whispers fill the verdant homes.
Among the moss, the worlds entwine,
Where every heart and soul align.

Twinkling Treetops

High above where giggles soar,
Canopies shift, a playful lore.
Swaying branches, bright and bold,
Dancing tales of joy unfold.

Leaves clap hands in breezy glee,
As critters share a secret spree.
A family of owls, wise and spry,
Shout jokes beneath the twilight sky.

Twinkling stars, they wink and tease,
Nights adorned with gentle breeze.
Chirps and croaks weave a song,
In treetops where we all belong.

With a rustle, the night takes flight,
As fireflies bloom, a sparkling sight.
Joy abounds in twinkling views,
Nature laughs with shades of blues.

Delightful Whispers of the Wilderness

In the heart of the woods, where secrets sway,
Trees exchange tales of their playful day.
A squirrel prances, with nuts he jests,
While branches chuckle, they rarely rest.

The brook gurgles on, with a bubbly cheer,
Echoing giggles that nature holds dear.
Fungi in circles, they dance on the ground,
While shadows shimmy, spinning around.

Sunbeams flicker like winks in the breeze,
Casting bright pranks among giggling leaves.
Mushrooms caper, a floral parade,
Whispers of laughter in every glade.

So step into this vibrant, wacky space,
Where every living thing dons a smiley face.
Nature's own jesters in a colorful spree,
Creating their humor, wild and free.

The Frothy Laughter of Pine

Pine trees sway, with a ticklish tease,
Their needles whisper fun with every breeze.
A squirrel darts past, wearing a grin,
As pine cones tumble, let the frolic begin!

Raindrops play drums on the forest floor,
Splattering jokes, then they're off for more.
The sun beamed bright with a giggling flair,
Making shadows dance, a lively affair.

Breezes blow jokes, a comical sound,
While acorns join in, rolling around.
The chipmunk chuckles, a quick little scamp,
As laughter echoes through every damp camp.

So join in the fun under pine's great crown,
Where humor blooms bright and never wears down.
With every rustle, you'll feel the delight,
In this forest frolic, everything feels right.

Timber Tales of Tickle

In timbered realms where giggles grew,
Trees share stories that are funny and new.
A woodpecker knocks, with a beat like a song,
While logs pipe up, saying, 'Come sing along!'

Leaves flutter down, like notes in a dance,
Spinning and swirling, inviting a chance.
A badger spills beans, with flair and with zest,
In this woodland circus, they're all at their best.

The bark cracks jokes, in a rugged old way,
While dew drops shimmer, like stars in the day.
Curly roots wiggle, in fits of delight,
Chortling amongst shadows, from morning to night.

So gather each tale, and let laughter swell,
In this timbered world, where jesters excel.
Every rustle and chuckle hails from afar,
Creating a chorus, like a sparkling star.

Glee Beneath the Leaves

Beneath the leaves, in a riot of green,
The giggles of creatures can often be seen.
A rabbit hops by, with a cheeky old leap,
While the owls snicker, laughing from sleep.

The flowers all stretch, blossoms quaking with mirth,
As sunbeams tickle the soil's warm birth.
Ladybugs dance, in a joyful parade,
While ferns flick their fronds, in a light-hearted charade.

Bees buzz with glee, carrying jokes in their hum,
As woodland folk gather, they know laughter's come.
With every rustle and flutter they hear,
The whole forest chuckles, a chorus so clear.

So dance with the shadows, let humor take flight,
In this merry woodland, everything's right.
With nature as host in this giggling spree,
Glee beneath the leaves is the place you should be.

Merriment in the Maple

In the canopy high, the branches sway,
Twisting and turning, they dance all day.
With whispers of giggles in breezy delight,
The maple leaves chuckle, a lively sight.

Beneath the bright sun, shadows prance,
Each rustle a riddle, a playful chance.
Squirrels scamper with joy in their hearts,
Playing hide and seek, wild little arts.

The sunlight dapples, like laughs in the air,
Nuts drop with a thud, bringing joy everywhere.
Gentle winds carry the whimsy so bright,
Nature's own comedy, a charming light.

With every soft gust, the branches confide,
The humor of life, too precious to hide.
In the arms of the maple, mirth finds a home,
Where memories flourish, and laughter can roam.

Smirking Stumps and Whimsical Woods

In the heart of the forest, the stumps wear a grin,
Each rings of age tell of secrets within.
Fungi like jesters caper around,
In the dance of the shadows, joy can be found.

The trails twist and turn, a curious maze,
Where whispers of mischief bring laughter ablaze.
Breezes come teasing, with tickles of glee,
The trees stand together, as merry as can be.

Branches are getting in whimsical fights,
Twirling their leaves in the soft, golden lights.
Bark is the canvas, with stories they weave,
Inside the stillness, where chuckles believe.

As night softly falls, the crickets will sing,
To the rhythm of joy that the forest will bring.
In stumps and in woods, where spirits come play,
The laughter of nature just brightens the day.

The Happy Echo of Trees

In the glen where the tall pines whisper and sway,
Echoes of joy seem to frolic and play.
The chirps of the birds send a cheeky reply,
As giggles of greenery flutter nearby.

Roots twist and turn, a tangle of fun,
In the shade of the boughs, the day's just begun.
A doe prances lightly, as if in a jest,
Among the wildflowers, she dances her best.

The leaves clap their hands in a shimmery cheer,
While each playful rustle brings magic near.
In the chorus of nature, there's laughter galore,
With every soft breeze, there's just more to explore.

As the sun dips below, and stars start to peep,
The echoes of trees join in laughter so deep.
A symphony made of mirth in the night,
The forest a stage, in its wondrous delight.

Jestful Vines Twining

Vines twist and twirl in a comedic embrace,
Wiggling their pages in the sun's warm face.
With sprightly enthusiasm, they leap and they climb,
Creating silly patterns, a jig in each rhyme.

Amidst the tall oaks, their laughter does weave,
Tales of two friends, who never will leave.
Each branch a companion, each leaf a delight,
In the tapestry of laughter, the world feels right.

Flowers peek out, with a smile in their glow,
Cheering on vines as they loop to and fro.
Nature's own jesters, in colors so bold,
Spreading the cheer in a festival told.

As dusk approaches softly, and shadows prolong,
The jest of the vines is a sweet, lively song.
In the heart of the garden, where joy intertwines,
The spirit of laughter forever enshrines.

The Merry Mirth of Moss

In the shade where the green moss grows,
Frogs practice their jests with a playful pose.
Whispers of humor in the breeze float,
As laughter rings out from a gnarled old coat.

Beneath the damp earth, the mushrooms giggle,
Tickling each other till they start to wiggle.
Their caps all a-quiver, they dance in delight,
While shadows join in for a whimsical night.

A squirrel in a hat spins stories with flair,
Telling all woodland friends, "Come if you dare!"
With nutty snacks as his trusty sidekick,
He juggles and tumbles, a mischievous trick.

The sun sets with joy, casting laughter to see,
Among softer whispers of jubilant glee.
Leaves rustle secrets of mirth in the trees,
In this merry moss kingdom, nobody flees.

Jolly Joints and Knots

Twisted trees weave tales in their crooked embrace,
Branching out boldly, with a jubilant grace.
Laughter erupts from their branches so spry,
As birds crackling jokes flutter high in the sky.

Knots twist together like friends in a brawl,
Sharing their wisps of humor, standing tall.
Breezes bring chuckles, tickling the leaves,
As nature's own comedians waggle and tease.

Boulders join in with a rollicking cheer,
Echoing laughter for all woods to hear.
In the merry chaos where whimsy takes flight,
Jolly joints chuckle, welcoming the night.

Roots twist below with a rib-tickling plan,
Unraveling stories from woodland to span.
With each knot that binds, there's a giggle to share,
In this quirky realm, everyone's filled with care.

The Bursting Laughter of Old Growth

Ancient trunks creak with a voice so profound,
Their stories of humor in whispers abound.
Gnarls and knots gather, a council of jest,
Sharing their secrets of merriment best.

Fungi pop up like clowns in a show,
Puffing out spores with a playful glow.
The moss wears a grin, full of wisdom to bare,
While echoes of laughter float sweet through the air.

Squirrels scamper like jesters on high,
Playing tricks on the owls with a wink of an eye.
Branches shake lightly as giggles take hold,
In the warmth of the moments, they shimmer like gold.

Nestled in shadows where sunlight can't roam,
The old growth erupts with a heartwarming poem.
Nature's own laughter, bountiful and bright,
In each bough that bends, there's a charming delight.

Grinning Guardians of the Wilderness

Sentinels standing with a twinkle and grin,
Guardians of woodlands where giggles begin.
Bark wraps around tales of merrymaking nights,
While twilight's laughter takes joyful flights.

Creaking branches towering, wisdom bestows,
Every rustle mutters a tale that just glows.
Rounding up creatures to join in the cheer,
The guardians chuckle, inviting all near.

From thickets to rivers, their giggles collide,
Echoing softly like ripples on tide.
Their roots tap-dance and the leaves smile bright,
Creating a wonderland sparkling with light.

In shrubby hallways adorned with fine jest,
Each twist tells a secret, every groove knows the best.
Through laughter and glee, they hold tight to the show,
These grinning guardians, forever aglow.

The Joyful Dance of the Dappled Leaves

In the breeze they twist and twirl,
Branches sway, a leafy whirl.
Sunlight glints on laughter bright,
Nature's giggles, pure delight.

Whispers tickle woodland ears,
Every rustle brings out cheers.
Squirrels wink and rabbits prance,
In this forest, all take a chance.

Jumpy shadows skip with glee,
Dancing circles, wild and free.
Frolics through the sunlit glade,
Where hearts are light, and woes do fade.

Endless fun beneath the boughs,
Playful antics make us bow.
Nature's jesters, bright and bold,
In this laughing grove, behold!

Chuckles in the Shade

Underneath the leafy crowns,
Where sunlight dips and gently frowns.
Mirthful breezes hum a tune,
Whispers dance beneath the moon.

Frogs in pond declare their fate,
Bubbles rising, oh so great!
Every ripple, a chuckle shared,
Nature's joy is not impaired.

Nestled here, we find the fun,
Silly shadows on the run.
Ants parade with tiny feet,
In this playful, shady beat.

Giggling leaves in playful sway,
Echo laughter, night and day.
With each rustle, joy awakes,
Heartfelt chuckles, nature makes!

The Laughter of Leafy Luminaries

Twinkling stars peek through the trees,
Crickets sing in rhythmic ease.
Emerald canopies delight,
A comedy in moonlit night.

Owls hoot jokes upon their perch,
While shadows play their nightly search.
Rustling leaves spill secrets bright,
Giggles weave through calm twilight.

Branches bow, a playful crew,
Nature's jesters, fresh and new.
Fireflies join with little winks,
Illuminating all in shrinks.

Beneath the glow of twinkling light,
Every giggle feels just right.
The forest breathes a joyful sound,
In leafy laughter, love is found.

Glee Among the Glens

In the glens, where breezes loom,
Flowers burst in vibrant bloom.
Petals giggle with delight,
Dancing softly in the light.

Meadows filled with joyous cries,
Butterflies in bright disguise.
Hopping bunnies bounce around,
In this playful, joyful ground.

Laughter spills from every nook,
Nature's joy, a happy book.
With each chirp, a comedic beat,
In this corner, life is sweet.

Swaying grass in sunny mirth,
Shares a secret of the earth.
In the glen, pure glee abounds,
As nature sings its funny sounds.

Mirth Amongst the Foliage

In the shade where shadows play,
Bright leaves wiggle, dance all day.
Squirrels chuckle, birds take flight,
Nature's jesters, pure delight.

Breezes tickle, branches sway,
Whispers, giggles in the fray.
Mushrooms grin, their caps so wide,
Funny faces, side by side.

Laughter echoes, soft and clear,
Echoes of the woodland cheer.
Roots entwined in jolly jest,
In this grove, we are the best.

Frogs jump high, a comic sound,
In this cradle, joy is found.
Every tree, a tale to tell,
In the woods, where spirits swell.

The Jolly Arboreal Symphony

Tiny critters leap and bound,
Upward, joy is all around.
With acorns dropping, laughter swells,
Nature's music, how it dwells.

Branches creak with playful cheer,
Wind in leaves whispers, 'Come near.'
Chirping choruses join the spree,
Filling forests, wild and free.

Twinkling stars wink from above,
As the night brings tales of love.
Crickets play their night-time tune,
Underneath a glowing moon.

Every rustle tells a joke,
Lively echoes, heartstrings yoke.
In the woods, such fun we find,
Joyful souls, forever kind.

Frolic in the Forest Canopy

Leaves like laughter in the breeze,
Jumpy critters tease with ease.
Upward climb, the branches twist,
In this game, none can resist.

Squirrels spin in wiggly lines,
Dancing as they chase the vines.
Sunlight sparkles, paint it gold,
Each tree a story, bright and bold.

Giggling streams through rocks they weave,
Every turn, a new reprieve.
Nature's canvas full of glee,
Where every day's a jubilee.

Frogs on lily pads, they sing,
In this realm, joy takes wing.
Amidst the greens, we chase our dreams,
In playful games, or so it seems.

Secrets of the Snickering Saplings

Tiny trunks in twisted plays,
Whisper secrets through the rays.
Buds that bloom with giggles bold,
Innocent humor, stories told.

Bouncing beams of sunlit paths,
Tickling shades and joyful laughs.
Rabbits hop, their antics free,
In this wood, pure ecstasy.

Breezes tease the leaves anew,
Nature's jesters, always true.
Swaying softly, they conspire,
Every rustle starts a fire.

Woodland friends with mischief gleam,
Filling each heart with a dream.
This merry band, wild and spry,
Underneath the endless sky.

Chortles in the Breeze

In the forest where shadows play,
Branches twist in a comical way,
Whispers dance with a giggling tease,
Nature's jokes flutter on the breeze.

Leaves rustle in laughter too loud,
Tickling trunks, they dance like a crowd,
Squirrels leap with a humorous flair,
Swinging and spinning through the air.

Mushrooms chuckle on mossy old stumps,
While beetles tap out their fun little thumps,
All around, a delightful scene,
Where chuckles erupt, and all is serene.

Breezes carry the laughs from afar,
Caressing the bark, like a soft guitar,
Every crack and creak tells a jest,
A woodland party, nature's best.

Merry Bark and Twigs

Bark in the sun wears a grin so wide,
Twisting and turning with nature as guide,
The forest floor's sprinkled with glee,
As sunlight plays on each playful tree.

Tiny twigs in a light-hearted race,
Jumping and bouncing with musical grace,
Nature's laughter in every nook,
Even the moss joins in the crook.

Branches sway, making shadows dance,
Inviting all critters to take a chance,
To hop and skip with joy so bright,
Under the stars, on a moonlit night.

Each root whispers tales old yet bold,
Of giggles and shenanigans yet untold,
A merry chorus, a woodland theme,
Where laughter plays, and dreams gleam.

Grins Beneath the Branches

Under the canopy, smiles are wide,
Branches cradle the joy inside,
With shadows that shimmer like gold,
Nature's humor never gets old.

Beneath the boughs, antics unfold,
Raccoons in masks, so brave and bold,
They skitter and play in a whimsical show,
Creating mischief wherever they go.

Each twig that bends tells a funny tale,
Of cheeky squirrels and a daring snail,
The dance of the leaves adds to the fun,
As daylight unfolds, life's just begun.

In this lively realm of blissful sights,
Laughter echoes, taking flight,
From roots to tips, contentment flows,
In every chuckle, the forest glows.

The Chuckling Grove

In the grove where giggles grow,
Every leaf has a tale to show,
Bark splits with joy, laughter rings,
Where twigs tell secrets on fluttering wings.

Frolicking foxes, noses a-quiver,
Romp through the grass, their spirits deliver,
Plays of pinches from hungry nests,
Unfolding warmth in nature's behests.

The wind joins in, tickling the pines,
Musical laughter in swirling lines,
A tapestry woven of playful delight,
Twilight brings giggles and shadows of night.

So linger awhile in this joking throng,
Where merriment echoes, and folks feel strong,
For in the chuckles, a bond we find,
As nature's joys leave the mundane behind.

The Cheerful Chronicles of Cedar

Once upon a time in the wood,
Tall trees shared tales, oh how they stood.
With branches waving cheerful and bright,
Spreading giggles from morning to night.

Squirrels danced in a playful spree,
Chasing their shadows, wild and free.
Whispers of joy rustled through leaves,
As sunlight tickled each bark that weaves.

A woodpecker drummed a catchy beat,
While rabbits hopped with nimble feet.
Mice told jokes in their cozy holes,
As laughter echoed through the knolls.

In this forest of chatter and cheer,
Every critter's joy was crystal clear.
The trees, with their wisdom, held the key,
To endless smiles, wild and carefree.

Nature's Quirky Chronicles

In a quirky grove where oddities bloom,
Bark wore hats, and foliage found room.
A raccoon in glasses read a tall tale,
While fireflies twinkled, leaving a trail.

The sunflowers giggled under the sky,
Shaking their heads as breezes waved by.
Ants planned a race on the forest floor,
Cheering for friends who wanted to score.

A wise old owl gave a wink and a nod,
While toads croaked jokes, the crowd just pawed.
Mushrooms wobbled with funny old tunes,
As laughter erupted beneath the moons.

Nature's stage, where the bizarre unfolds,
Each blossom and branch with a story it holds.
With each funny twist, the world came alive,
In this land of the strange, we all thrive.

Amused Roots in the Earth

Down where the roots giggle and sigh,
Tiny critters play, oh my, oh my!
Worms wear hats made of leaves and clover,
While beetles roll dice as they lean over.

The daisies don bows and perform ballet,
As the brook sings tunes that lead the way.
A mole tells tales that make everyone cheer,
With giggles and chuckles that float through the sphere.

Tails pinch cheeks; the grass tickles toes,
Each little creature in laughter glows.
Underground parties with music and cheer,
Bring warmth and joy for all creatures near.

In this hug of roots, where chuckles abound,
Life's simple pleasures play all around.
With each tiny laugh that springs from the earth,
A treasure of humor and joy finds its berth.

The Playful Patterns of Bark

In a grove of patterns where humor unfolds,
The bark tells stories as each tree beholds.
A jester among branches dressed in green,
Makes every visitor burst at the seams.

Vines twirl and twist, dancing in the breeze,
As nature calls forth its playful decrees.
Ladybugs giggle, butterflies spin,
In this forest of laughter, joy finds its kin.

Gnarled knots grin with secrets they keep,
As rabbits jump circles and tumble in heaps.
The wind sings a tune, flutes made of leaves,
Painting smiles on the bark that believes.

With colors so bright and a whimsical spark,
Each nook of the wood sings a lighthearted lark.
In laughter's embrace, together they thrive,
In this symphony of nature, all feel alive.

Jests in the Forest Shadows

In the woods where whispers play,
Mossy trunks tell tales each day.
Branches sway with a silly dance,
Nature's jesters, lost in chance.

Beneath the boughs, critters scheme,
A raccoon's prank, a squirrel's dream.
Laughter rings through leafy beams,
Echoes of their playful themes.

Logs in a line, a grand parade,
Mimic the tales the forest made.
Rain drops tap in a rhythmic beat,
Nature's laughter, oh so sweet.

In shadows deep, secrets unfold,
With every knot, a story told.
Join the fun, let your spirit soar,
In the woods, we'll laugh some more.

Giggles of the Aged Timber

Old trees chuckle, roots entwined,
Worn bark holds stories of the kind.
Branches croon with a creaky tune,
Dancing softly under the moon.

Twisted limbs weave silly tales,
While breezes mimic their playful gales.
A gnome winks from his wooden perch,
As woodland sprites begin their search.

Sunshine dapples, the shadows bounce,
Bark cracks up, and the leaves renounce.
Squirrels giggle, and chipmunks cheer,
In the forest, joy's always near.

With every ring, a laugh's unveiled,
Chronicles of jokes never failed.
Nature's humor, both rich and grand,
In the heart of each ancient land.

Smiles in the Sunlight

Sunbeams dance on the forest floor,
Each leaf's glimmer invites us to explore.
The wind whispers jests with the light,
In this realm, everything feels just right.

Frogs leap forth with a playful croak,
While tiny bugs try to share a joke.
Flower petals sway with glee,
In this bright world, we're all carefree.

Little creatures prance without fear,
Every rustle brings laughter near.
The bark of a tree grins wide,
With each chuckle, joy won't hide.

Under the sun, we play and roam,
With vibrant smiles, we feel at home.
Nature hums a sweet refrain,
In this merry place, there's no pain.

Playful Rings of History

Each ring in wood, a joke long spun,
Whispers of laughter since time begun.
Logs stacked high, a sight to see,
Each story told, a memory.

With every grain, a chuckle grows,
Secrets held tight, only nature knows.
Elders share in the soft breeze sigh,
In the shade, time laughs as it passes by.

As shadows stretch, the twilight sings,
Chirping crickets join in the flings.
The dance of shadows, a joyous sight,
Nature's jesters in the fading light.

So gather round, let us cheer,
For history's humor brings us near.
In the woods, we share this bliss,
With each moment, how can we miss?

The Bark of Bliss

In a forest so wild and free,
Trees whisper secrets with glee.
Branches sway, a merry dance,
Nature's jest, a playful chance.

Saplings giggle in the breeze,
Tickling leaves with utmost ease.
Trunks stand tall with a grin wide,
As shadows play and sprites abide.

With squirrels prancing on each limb,
Their capers make the sunlight dim.
A woodpecker plays a silly beat,
While lizards shuffle on small feet.

Amidst the hues of green and brown,
Laughter echoes all around.
Each rustle tells a cheerful joke,
The forest is a fun-filled cloak.

Jestful Journeys Among the Boughs

Adventurers roam with hearts so light,
Swinging through branches, a thrilling sight.
Logs snicker at every leap,
While the woodland seems to peep.

In the hollow, a wise old tree,
Shares tales of antics, wild and free.
With knots that chuckle, trunks that sway,
They dance along the sunny ray.

As frolicking foxes dash and dive,
Nature's spirit comes alive.
The breeze whistles a cheeky tune,
Guiding wanderers 'neath the moon.

Every step a tender jest,
Among the boughs, all feel their best.
With every sound a playful nudge,
In this forest, no one can grudge.

The Rambunctious Roots

Buried deep in the earth's embrace,
Roots prance around in their wild space.
Twisting, turning like they're in jest,
Each tangle's a riddle, a burst of zest.

They tickle the soil, a sneaky game,
As flowers bubble with laughter's flame.
Beneath the surface, they wiggle and squirm,
Creating chaos, an earthy term.

The moles giggle at their playful art,
While worms wiggle and take part.
A jigsaw puzzle of giggly glee,
In every nook, a hidden spree.

Through the forest, this mischief spreads,
With every shuffle, the humor spreads.
These rambunctious roots, entwined and bold,
Create a tale that never gets old.

Nature's Giddy Riddles

In the sway of branches, riddles unfold,
Nature's laughter is a joy to behold.
Each rustle of leaves a puzzle to share,
Inviting all creatures with playful flair.

A butterfly flutters, a riddle in flight,
Her wings whisper secrets, shining bright.
The stones chuckle, they know the score,
While crickets sing riddles forevermore.

Mountains chuckle, with valleys that grin,
With every breeze, a new game begins.
The sun peeks through, a cheeky laugh,
Drawing wild shapes on a sunny path.

In the heart of the woods, where fun reigns supreme,
Nature's giddy riddles weave a dream.
Every sound, every stir in the air,
Is a merry jest, expect it to share.

Sprigs of Smiles

In the forest, giggles gleam,
Branches sway in a playful dream.
Bubbly brooks hum tunes so bright,
Nature's jesters in morning light.

Squirrels play tag in the trees,
Chasing sunbeams with such ease.
Rustling leaves burst into song,
A symphony where all belong.

Mushrooms caper in the shade,
Creating games that never fade.
Jolly winds twirl the weeds,
Whispering secrets through the seeds.

Laughter echoes from afar,
As crickets play their tiny guitar.
The world spins with a joyful cheer,
In every nook, the fun is near.

The Merry Whistle of Nature

Whistles dance on the breeze,
Tickling the grass and trees.
Every creature joins the play,
In a merry, wild array.

Bumblebees buzz with delight,
Painting colors with their flight.
Dancing petals swirl and sway,
In a wiggly, twinkly way.

The giggly brook hops along,
Singing stanzas of a song.
Frogs croak in a comic tone,
Nature's jesters, never alone.

Underneath a sky so blue,
Joyful antics come in view.
Every rustle, every sound,
Brings the humor all around.

Lighthearted Leaves

Leaves flip and flop in the air,
Tickled by a breezy affair.
Nature chuckles, full of grace,
In this whimsical, grassy space.

Dandelions blow puffed seeds,
Carrying laughs like little beads.
Breezes whisper jokes so sly,
As fluffy clouds parade on high.

Twigs twist in a silly dance,
Inviting all to take a chance.
Swaying flowers join the spree,
Bouncing with unbridled glee.

Caterpillars spin their tales,
While ladybugs wear tiny veils.
The forest hums a joyful beat,
In the sunshine, life is sweet.

The Dulcet Dance of the Driftwood

Driftwood winks on the shore,
Telling tales forevermore.
With every wave, it sways around,
Highlighting joy where smiles abound.

Sea grasses giggle in the tide,
Soaking up the playful ride.
Barnacles clap in a warm embrace,
As salty breezes quicken the pace.

Barn owls hoot in a tender jest,
While sunlit waves invite a rest.
Seagulls swoop with a gleeful caw,
Nature's humor breaks every law.

On this stage where winds convene,
The driftwood laughs at sights unseen.
With every splash, a chuckle's tossed,
In a world where joy is never lost.

Witty Woodlands

In the woods where the squirrels play,
The branches wiggle, come what may.
The old oak leans, a joke to tell,
While pine trees chuckle, feeling swell.

The leaves all whisper, in breezy glee,
As chipmunks race to climb a tree.
A fox runs by, all in a dash,
Tripping over roots with quite a crash.

The mushrooms giggle, brighten the floor,
While hedgehogs snicker, roaming their shore.
Each creature shares a wink and grin,
In this woodland where fun begins.

So journey here, where jests take flight,
In verdant realms where day meets night.
With every step and rustling leaf,
Find joy in nature, beyond belief.

The Joyous Dance of Diligent Dew

Early morn, the droplets glow,
Dancing on petals, putting on a show.
They jiggle lightly, with gentle flair,
While breezes giggle, twirling in air.

A ladybug joins with playful spins,
As ants march by with cheeky grins.
The sun peeks in, to catch the sight,
Of gleeful drops that sparkle bright.

The grass beneath hums a merry tune,
As dew drops shimmer under the moon.
Together they twist in a silly ballet,
In a garden where laughter holds sway.

So come, step lightly on this bright stage,
Join the fun, forget your age.
In each droplet's joyful embrace,
Find the whispers of this happy place.

The Raucous Regal Redwoods

In the shadow of giants, tall they rise,
With bark so thick, like nature's guise.
The whispers of winds begin to tease,
And branches sway with effortless ease.

A clamor of creatures fills the air,
As raccoons bicker without a care.
The owls hoot jokes from the highest perch,
While squirrels scatter, their antics a search.

The sunlight spills, a golden hue,
As shadows dance in a jig so true.
In the crown of trees, there's laughter so grand,
A raucous symphony from nature's band.

So gather here with mirth and cheer,
Amongst the tall trunks, joy is near.
For in mighty woods, where laughter grows,
You'll find glee blooming like a rose.

The Joyride of Bark

On a warm day, bark gleams with pride,
Riding the winds, it takes a stride.
With each knot and twist, a tale unfolds,
Of playful times and secret holds.

A chipmunk leans on a sturdy limb,
While beetles march, their chances slim.
The breeze ruffles through the leafy crew,
As nature laughs, in vibrant hue.

The sun tickles bark, in warm embrace,
With stories shared, in timeless space.
The laughter rolls through the forest wide,
On this jovial journey, we joyously glide.

So come along, and join the ride,
In the merry woods where giggles hide.
For in every groove, and every mark,
You'll find the joy in the happy bark.

Whimsical Whispers of the Wild

In the depths of the woodland, a giggle takes flight,
Trees sway and chuckle, in the soft, gentle light.
A squirrel with a grin dances round a tall oak,
Mischief in the air, with each playful joke.

Beneath the bright leaves, a rustle and cheer,
A bird on a branch sings, spreading joy near.
The bark has a smile, the roots tap their toes,
Nature's own laughter, in harmony flows.

Raccoons in the moonlight, with antics so sly,
Jokes weave through the branches, they tumble and fly.
Each flower's bright laughter, a petal's soft song,
In a world full of whimsy, where all will belong.

The dew-drops are chuckles, the sunbeams all beam,
In this playful forest, all life feels like a dream.
With each moment of joy, the trees come alive,
In the whispers of wild, where giggles revive.

Twinkling Tones of the Timbers

Under a canopy bright, where laughter still grows,
Timbers share tales, as the cool breezes do blow.
A chipmunk spins round, with a hat made of twigs,
Twirling with joy, he jigs and he digs.

The leaves join the fun, rustling soft in delight,
As branches create shadows, dancing with the light.
A stream with a chuckle flows swiftly along,
Mimicking voices in a playful, sweet song.

Frogs wear tiny crowns, while crickets play tunes,
Nature puts on a show, beneath glowing moons.
Each pulse of the forest brings smiles galore,
With spirits unbroken, the laughter will soar.

So if you seek joy, in the woods take a stroll,
Find giggles in breezes, and let your heart roll.
As twinkling tones echo through timber and leaf,
The essence of fun hides away in belief.

Whispers of the Woodland

Beneath the tall boughs where the roots intertwine,
    Whispers of laughter seep sweetly, divine.
  A hedgehog snickers as he rolls on the ground,
    With echoes of giggles, everywhere found.

  The sunbeams dribble through branches above,
    Sprinkling warmth, like a soft joyful hug.
    Every bud bursts with stories untold,
  While wise trees creak softly, with humor bold.

    A fox with a grin, weaves in and out fast,
    Dancing to rhythms of the wild, unsurpassed.
  The moss on the rocks looks up with a gleam,
  In a woodland of laughter, all beings can dream.

    Together they play, this enchanting array,
Where whispers of woodland chase worries away.
    In every sweet rustle, find joy is the rule,
    For nature's a jester, with laughter as fuel.

The Giggling Canopy

High up in the branches where the leaves twist and sway,
A canopy giggles, brightening the day.
With each soft rustle, a joke fills the air,
Chirping and chuckling, without a single care.

The sunbeams peek in, with a wink and a smile,
Bouncing on boughs like a playful child's style.
Birds join in chorus, their tunes full of cheer,
Creating a symphony, sweet music we hear.

A squirrel with antics, hops high up the trunk,
While down below, mushrooms hide giggles in funk.
Joy flows through the forest, a curious game,
With nature as actor, and laughter the name.

So wander the pathways, let spirits run free,
In the giggling canopy, where all want to be.
Every whisper and rustle, a tickle of sound,
In this playful paradise, pure joy can be found.

Radiant Laughter from the Roots

Beneath the soil, where whispers creep,
The roots exchange secrets, silent and deep.
Tiny critters clamor, each with a jest,
Nature's playful spirit, never at rest.

Sunlight tickles leaves, dancing in glee,
Branches sway gently, like waves in the sea.
The forest erupts, a riot of cheer,
As laughter resonates, vibrant and clear.

Blossoms burst forth in colors so bright,
Each petal a giggle, pure delight.
A breeze joins in, with a mischievous sigh,
In this merry theater, time flutters by.

Nature's enchantment, a humorous weave,
Hiding in shadows, the playful reprieve.
Every bark holds a tale, a quirky delight,
In the heart of the woods, joy takes flight.

Brink of the Barking Birth

At dawn, the trees tell stories anew,
Barking with laughter, the forests pursue.
A symphony rises, branches all tune,
Each rustle a riddle beneath the bright moon.

Roots interlock, a tangle of dreams,
Nature's old spirits whisper in beams.
Nuts chuckle softly, while acorns poke fun,
From tiniest seeds, the business begun.

Frogs take the stage, with leaps and with bounds,
Creating a show with their ribbiting sounds.
Squirrels stand tall, with nuts held in pride,
Winking at passersby, never to hide.

The air full of mischief, the wild things unite,
In this comedy of life, everything's right.
Trees sway and giggle, their leaves in a spin,
On the brink of the birthing, where joy does begin.

Chuckles of the Elder Trees

Ancient giants, oh, how they chuckle,
Roots entwined, in a merry huddle.
Bark worn with wisdom, stories to lend,
Echoing laughter, a brush with a friend.

Their branches sway low, bowing with mirth,
Tickling the air, celebrating their birth.
With each passing breeze, giggles take flight,
In a timeless dance, from morn until night.

Whimsical shadows flicker and flit,
Creatures gather round, joining in wit.
The forest, a tapestry, woven with gleam,
Elder trees giggle in a spilled-over dream.

Beneath canopies vast, where jokes never cease,
Nature's delight flows like a river of peace.
With every rustle, their chuckles convene,
In the heart of the woods, where laughter is seen.

The Frolicsome Heart of Forests

In the frolicsome heart where the wild things play,
Trees sway and twirl, dancing the day away.
With branches outstretched like arms in the air,
The forest is filled with giggles laid bare.

Dancing in circles, the flowers react,
Tickled by breezes, they humorously act.
Each petal a dancer, swaying with grace,
In this jovial jungle, there's always a space.

Bushes burst forth with laughter so bold,
Budding up jokes in a tale yet untold.
The melody rises, a whimsical song,
As nature herself humors, all day long.

Creatures abound, with mischief in sight,
Chasing their shadows from morning till night.
In the frolicsome heart, joy echoes anew,
A celebration of life, forever in view.

Forest Frolics in the Evening Light

Amid the trees where shadows play,
The quirky sprites like to sway.
Branches bend with a gentle chuckle,
As leaves flutter in a merry shuffle.

Beneath the bark, a tiny joke,
Two squirrels giggle as they poke.
Acorns rolling like comical dice,
In this woodland where all is nice.

The twilight whispers a secret grin,
Nature hums with a joyful spin.
Evening light paints the scene bright,
Where every branch holds pure delight.

So come and tread this merry trail,
Where laughter dances, never stale.
With each step, feel the joy ignite,
In the forest frolics of the night.

Giggles from the Grainy Grove

In the grove where mischief breeds,
Funny creatures sprout like weeds.
Mossy rocks with jolly grins,
Turning frowns to silly spins.

Bumbles of bees in a playful race,
Buzzing by with a cheeky face.
Tangled vines weave a wiggly dance,
In this place where giggles prance.

Sunlight filters through leaves so bright,
Casting humor in the golden light.
The trees sway gently, whispering cheer,
Inviting all who wander near.

As shadows stretch in the fading sun,
Every creature shares the fun.
In every corner of this space,
The grainy grove wears a smiling face.

Jovial Shadows of the Timberland

Timberland tales spin in the air,
Where laughter hides without a care.
Frogs croak jokes on lily pads,
While chipmunks cheer on their silly fads.

Beneath tall pines, a riddle sways,
Mirthful echoes fill the days.
Swaying ferns share secrets in blue,
Each whisper tickles, a comedic cue.

With every breeze comes a peal of joy,
Where laughter is free, no need for ploy.
Nature's jesters roam wild and bold,
In this timberland where tales unfold.

Dappled shadows weave a funny quilt,
With every moment, warmth is built.
Join the frolic, take a chance,
In jovial shades, let spirits dance.

Chronicles of the Cheery Canopy

Under the canopy, stories bloom,
With giggles bubbling in every room.
Sunbeams tickle the branches high,
While birds exchange a comedic sigh.

Wind whispers tales of playful jest,
As each tree stands tall in its best.
Frolicking shadows skip and race,
In this haven of endless grace.

Chirpy crickets play their tunes,
Bouncing to the light of the moons.
Furry friends gather in a row,
Sharing secrets that only they know.

Chronicles ripe with laughter unfold,
Every leaf gleaming like gold.
So stay awhile, embrace the cheer,
In this cheery canopy, joy is near.

Ridiculous Roots

Beneath the trees, they wiggle and sway,
Roots in a tangle, they scheme all day.
Snatching up whispers, the ground starts to grin,
As dirt-stuffed giggles burst forth from within.

With boots made of bark, they trip on their toes,
A dance of the silly, where nobody knows.
They tumble and fumble, around they will spin,
Each stumble a joke, each fall is a win.

Ribbons and branches high five in the breeze,
Chasing the shadows with giggles and tease.
They tickle the soil with roots full of cheer,
And bring forth the laughter that all love to hear.

Through twists and turns, let the fun freely flow,
In the heart of the forest, just watch it all go.
Nature's own jesters in green, brown, and gold,
Their antics a tale, forever retold.

The Gleeful Timberfolk

In the heart of the wood, where the laughter runs wild,
The timberfolk dance, like a giggling child.
With caps made of moss and their shoes made of vine,
They skip through the ferns, adding sparkle and shine.

Chirps from the critters weave songs in the air,
As branches sway gently, trapping joy everywhere.
With each step they take, trees chuckle with glee,
The forest alive with pure camaraderie.

They juggle the cones, making faces so fun,
Crafting stories and pranks 'til the day is all done.
The glade is a stage, under sunbeams that prance,
Inviting all creatures to join in the dance.

So listen, dear friend, to the sylvan delight,
As timberfolk twirl under starlight so bright.
In laughter, they thrive, our whimsical crew,
Bringing joy to the earth, and to all, they imbue.

Delightful Dances in the Glade

In the glade where the sunshine like sparkles falls down,
Creatures convene for a merrymaking crown.
The squirrels play fiddles, the rabbits reply,
With twirls and with leaps, they reach up to the sky.

Breezes become partners, swirling round and around,
As mushrooms play drums on the soft, mossy ground.
Each flap of a wing adds a beat to the cheer,
Creating a symphony only they hear.

The shadows grow longer, but spirits stay high,
As sunlight winks gently while shadows comply.
With every soft giggle, the trees seem to sway,
Celebrating the rafts of laughter that play.

So join in the fun, let your heart take a chance,
In the glade full of joy, come and join in the dance.
Where every small step turns to cheerful parade,
In the blissful embrace of the fun-loving glade.

Whimsy Woven in Wood

In a forest of wonders, where mischief takes root,
Wooden shenanigans make everyone hoot.
With branches that wiggle and twigs that go snap,
The trees hold a conference, planning a trap.

The owls in their wisdom just chuckle away,
As pinecones play tricks on the beams of the day.
They tumble like children on soft forest floor,
Where whimsical spirits come calling for more.

Knots in the bark bubble up with a laugh,
Telling tall tales in the twilight's soft half.
With playful glee, they twist and they sprawl,
Creating a tapestry, humor for all.

So come take a stroll through this jolly parade,
Where nature spins stories that never do fade.
The whimsy is woven in wood, leaf, and vine,
In this grove of delight, every moment's divine.

Giggles of the Grains

In fields where shadows play,
The stalks begin to sway,
They whisper silly things,
As breezes dance and bring.

A tumbleweed skips by,
With a twinkle in its eye,
It rolls along the ground,
In laughter, joy is found.

The daisies nod their heads,
While poppies share their threads,
In every sway and twine,
A joyous, jolly line.

So skip across the land,
With nature's merry band,
In golden waves so bright,
The grains bring pure delight.

Bark's Hidden Humor

Upon the trees so tall,
Their bark reveals it all,
With faces carved by time,
They chuckle, oh so fine.

Gnarled roots in the ground,
Share secrets all around,
In knots and twists they play,
With each and every sway.

Branches stretch like arms,
With their funny little charms,
They tickle passing skies,
As clouds go tumbling by.

Amongst the leafy crowd,
The nature spirits loud,
With every crevice seen,
A humor evergreen.

Echoes of Amusement in the Grove

In a grove where laughter rings,
The wind speaks of silly things,
Shadows dance beneath the light,
A joyous, playful sight.

The squirrels play a prank,
On all who pass the plank,
With acorns flying high,
As giggles fill the sky.

The sunbeams wink and beam,
Creating a whimsical dream,
While every leaf will sway,
In their bright and cheery way.

So come and join the fun,
As shadows stretch and run,
In nature's giddy throng,
Where echoes laugh along.

The Jests of Ancient Trees

In ancient woods they stand,
With roots deep in the land,
Their branches wave and tease,
With whispers of the breeze.

Each ring a tale retold,
Of mischief bold and gold,
Their canopies bestow,
A laugh with every blow.

The owls roll their eyes,
At jokes beneath the skies,
While shadows slip and glide,
With every laughter wide.

So gather round the trees,
With all their jolly tease,
In a place where giggles swell,
And every story's swell.

Joyful Resonance of Leaves

In the breeze they dance and sway,
Whispers of joy in green ballet.
Tickling the branches, a soft refrain,
Nature's giggles, a sweet champagne.

Rustling softly, the jokes they share,
As sunlight filters, a warm affair.
The canopy chuckles, a playful tease,
A canopy of mirth, the swaying trees.

Each leaf a voice in the cheerful hum,
With every rustle, the fun beats drum.
On this stage of vibrant hues,
The forest revels in its own muse.

A symphony of green, a merry show,
With laughter echoing, to and fro.
The joyous cadence of woodland wit,
In every corner, where spirits sit.

The Lively Laughter of Underbrush

Beneath the boughs, the world is bright,
Chasing shadows in sheer delight.
With every poke, a giggle bare,
Whiskers of whimsy fill the air.

Frisky sprouts in a crowded zone,
With playful pranks they're all alone.
They tickle travelers, sweep their feet,
A jovial game beneath the heat.

Curly ferns in a cheerful twist,
With every touch, it's hard to resist.
The underbrush chuckles, alive with cheer,
As adventurers stumble, drawing near.

In the heart of green, surprises bloom,
Each step forward brings glee and zoom.
A realm of laughter, this woodland space,
Bubbling joy, nature's warm embrace.

Ticklish Twigs

Twigs twist and bend, a playful sight,
In the gentle breeze, they take flight.
A poke, a prod, a merry squeak,
In their funny language, they speak.

From cracks and creaks, the stories rise,
Of feathery frolics 'neath clear blue skies.
With every snap, a trick is played,
They echo laughter in their parade.

The branches tease with jiggles galore,
Creating moments that we adore.
With every sway, the giggles grow,
In nature's gallery, the twigs put on a show.

Whispering secrets, they never tire,
Their silly shuffles set hearts afire.
In the wild, where the fun unfolds,
Ticklish twigs share stories bold.

Sprightly Shadows

Shadows play in the dappled light,
Frolicking freely, a pure delight.
With each flicker, they bounce and tease,
Dancing around like a playful breeze.

As sunlight weaves through the branches bare,
Patterns of joy fill the open air.
The ground giggles 'neath the merry hats,
Of playful shadows, like friendly chats.

Chasing the sun, they flit and sway,
A game of tag 'til the end of day.
In the twilight, secrets start to bloom,
Echoes of laughter of shadows loom.

Sprightly silhouettes with stories to share,
Filling the world with a whimsical air.
In the quietude, the joy holds tight,
As shadows charm the softly falling night.

The Rapture of Rustic Retreats

In the woods where shadows play,
A tree stump dances, come what may.
Whispers tickle branches high,
As squirrels giggle, never shy.

Mushrooms caper in a line,
Chasing sunlight, seeking wine.
With every breeze, a chuckle peaks,
Nature's jest in rustling creeks.

Frogs wear hats, a quirky style,
Jumping jests that make us smile.
The owls wink with silly eyes,
In this haven, laughter flies.

When moonlight beams, they sing a tune,
Crickets beat the night in June.
Wooden giants sway with glee,
In this patch of fantasy.

Wondrous Whimsy in the Woods

Dancing branches twist and twirl,
With every spin, they laugh and whirl.
Hopping hares join in the craze,
While chipmunks stare in a daze.

A ticklish breeze ruffles the leaves,
Tickling thoughts in playful eves.
The bark seems to grin wide and bright,
In this realm of pure delight.

Little critters throw a ball,
Frogs leap high to heed the call.
Laughter floats from tree to tree,
Echoing wild and fancy-free.

Giggling streams bubble and splash,
Nature's party, a joyous bash.
Underneath a giggling sky,
Miracles bloom, and hopes can fly.

Joysparked by the Jamboree of Trees

In the meadow, humor grows,
With breezy tales and silly shows.
Woodpeckers drum a merry beat,
While bunnies hop on tiny feet.

Branches shake with teasy grace,
As sunlight beams on every face.
Caterpillars spin their yarns,
In a world of magic charms.

Hats on heads of dreamy deer,
Hear them share their laughter near.
The trees sway, join in the fun,
While moonlight sparkles, day is done.

With the night, the giggles rise,
Underneath the starlit skies.
Forests hum their happy tune,
Nature's jest beneath the moon.

The Snickering Canopy

Up in the branches, secrets hide,
Echoed giggles, wild and wide.
Leafy listeners sway and sway,
　Telling tales at close of day.

Tiny bugs with shiny hats,
Dancing 'round like playful spats.
The air is thick with whispered cheer,
In this realm, there's naught to fear.

Squirrels play tag, they zip and dash,
Creating storms of leaves that crash.
Every rustle, a chuckle shared,
In this haven where joy's declared.

Under the dome, stars begin to peek,
In a tapestry where chic critters speak.
Nature's laughter, soft and sweet,
A playful world, where all hearts meet.

www.ingramcontent.com/pod-product-compliance
Lightning Source LLC
Chambersburg PA
CBHW051630160426
43209CB00004B/584